1

Untangling Success

6 Key Principles To Having Whatever The Heck You Want!

Untangling Success: 6 Key Principles To Having Whatever The Heck You Want!

First Published in 2019 by

Tj Atkinson

ACKNOWLEDGEMENTS

I wish to dedicate this book to my parents, who have been my everlasting supporters throughout my turbulent journey as an entrepreneur and have always supported me even through my crazy decisions. I am eternally grateful for teaching me that I could accomplish anything and everything I set my heart to.

Finally, I would like to thank you for picking up this book and trusting me to share my experiences, my insights, and my heart with you so you can fulfil your dreams and goals. I am grateful.

Life is harsh! Get over it!

Content Page

Who this book is for

If you bought this book because you wanted a nice, song and dance kind of book that is going to make you feel great about your current situation, then do yourself a favour right now and throw the book in the bin or burn it to ashes. This book couldn't be further from comfortable. To be fair, I would be surprised if you get to chapter II.

It is because, this book is certainly not going to make you feel warm and fuzzy but will challenge you to grow and take some serious action that will push you to new heights.

If you are happy to face some uncomfortable truths and take some much needed action in order to catapult your growth, then please read on.

You have been lied to. So throughout the course of this book, I aim to tell you some liberating truths.

Some of you will be able to handle it and face some of your fears and truths head on, while many of you will run away and revert back to the old life that you wished you could escape from but refuse to escape.

If you are stuck, it's your fault!

Knock, Knock

Who's there?

Success?

Success who?

If you don't know who the heck I am, how are you supposed to acquire me?

"Uh, Houston, we've had a problem"

What is right in front you but you just can't seem to attain it?

My mentor once dramatically tied an apple to a string, dangled it above my head and told me not to move my legs or arms but to take a bite out of the floating apple. Every time I seemed close to taking a bite, he yanked the apple higher and this carried on for a further 5 minutes. Eventually, he laughed and said, "success is like a floating apple, when you think you are just about to take a bite, the requirements always change". I hated him, but he was right. Success is not a straight, brightly illuminated road, but a narrow, unlit street with no RAC or AA vehicles to tow you to the nearest safety point if your car breaks down.

He rounded up our meeting and gave me 3 pieces of advice

1. Always think inside out.
   (If there is a problem, it's is probably your fault, go and figure it out)

2. Treat success as you would treat a woman
   (Once you understand women, then you are one step closer to understanding success. Which means you will forever be a student)

3. Cover all angles
   (Always think 2 or 3 steps ahead) Your ability to see around the corner is your superpower.

Did I feel silly gnashing my teeth against the unattainable apple? Yes but I learnt two very significant lessons.

Firstly, apples are good for you, but more seriously, success is right in front of us, yet the only reason some people manage to take a bite and others are left gnashing their teeth in thin air is just one difference.

Perspective!

<u>'Uh, Houston, we've had a problem'.</u>

Your perspective in life will determine how you deal with or approach an issue.

As I exited, he said "hey Tj, you love women don't ya. Try this, think about success as if she was the woman of your dreams.

She is fierce, she is bold, she is beautiful but she is also fed up of half-arsed, lazy men who do the same thing and say the same things that every other man has said to her.

If you want to woo her you, change the way you think!"

Introduction

For the purpose of this book, let us say success is the wo[man] of your dreams.

[S]he is going to share with you, the secrets on how to successfully woo he[r].

Success is elusive. She evades her pursuant, yet she freely surrenders to those who woo her correctly.

There are keys to unlocking the free gift of success, yet many of us fail to discover these keys and thus fail to open the doors to abundance, wealth and success.

In this book, I am going to challenge you to look at how to attain success in a slightly different way.

Some will be controversial, some of the methodology might strain you, some of them will cause you to introspect and challenge you to try things you didn't know you could do.

But I guarantee you this. If you follow the steps and systems prescribed in the following chapters, you will woo over success and everything you have ever dreamed or desired will be yours.

"Do one thing every day that scares you."

Anonymous

Chapter One
You are designed for success! NOT!

"Success loves mind games. She says, if you want to find her, you have to learn to trick your brain".

You are destined for greatness
You are designed to be successful
You are destined to succeed

No you are not!

As fancy as these statements may sounds and as fluffy and soul-stirring as they might come across, the truth is the complete opposite. You are not destined to succeed. You are not designed to be great.

In fact, you are designed to fail! That might have come across a bit harsh, but I wanted to punch you in the face soon as possible. I wanted to give you an authentic dose of what it will truly require, if you embark on this journey unwittingly. I want to wake you up the reality of how difficult attaining success really is and what it really require to court her.

Success is available to all, who simply develop the ability to woo her.

She is a dancing damsel, free in nature, cascading across the earth, wrecking ships, destroying hopes, drowning dreams, but all she really desires is someone that knows how to handle her; a stern hand, an unwavering pursuant, who is also willing to dine in the fire with her. She willingly rewards the few, who are willing to stake it all on taming her.

The issue is that most of us have been wooing her wrongly. We have flirted, skirted around, made subtle advances, but failed to put our heads in the lion's mouth. We fail to accept that she is a mighty queen, that raises but also lowers. A monarch who elevates but also demotes. The journey to attaining success is a long, harsh, cold road.

How can you capture something you do not know? I am elusive, I am exclusive, I am wild, I bless, I curse, I destroy, I restore. I am and can be whatever you want me to be. But I am certainly not easy to attain.

This shocking news will cause 99% of readers to say "well, what's the flipping point of reading the rest book, if you say I'm pretty much doomed already?"

To answer your question. I didn't write this book to give you a warm, fuzzy, cuddly feeling that will further gaslight you to thinking everyone can be successful. I wrote this book to give you some facts, some ideas and some truths that will invariably separate the ones that truly desire success from the ones hiding in the shadow and simply peeing in the wind.

Secondly, you are doomed, but there are a few controversial and debatable things that you can still do that will help you tame success. The ideas I have noted in this book, are not for everyone. So, if you are not willing to try something that might be a little different from the 'stuff' you have been doing before, that hasn't yielded you much results, then BURN this book or throw it away.

This is your first opportunity to bow out now. You are unlikely to make it! You are unlikely to succeed. I won't take offence if you burn this book to ashes. It just further reiterates my point, that maybe, just maybe you don't have what it takes to succeed. But, if you are still reading, you might just have something in you that will take you the distance.

I flipping hate gurus! Their prescriptions and anecdotes for success, have played a part in us not attaining our success. I understand, we all need to be cajoled and motivated, however, sometimes someone needs to hold our faces to the fire and tell us some damn truths. "You are destined for success!", they shout, "you are great!" they bellow, and you buy into it. Yet, it's a false and destructive narrative. The idea of a pre-disposition to success is one reason why most people never achieve success. Success does not belong to anyone. She is a wildflower that blossoms as she pleases, a gust of wind that blow as she desires. She floats around looking for the brave and diligent that can tame her. It is simply there to be taken by those who know how.

If you want to be successful, you must capture success and in order to capture success, it requires strategy.

There are keys to capturing success yet only a handful of people will ever discover the tools.

It is '**achieved**' through the '**process**' of '**effort**'.

Let's consider those three important words for a moment

Achieve - To get or attain as the result of **exertion.**

Process - A series of **actions** taken in order to achieve a goal.

Effort - A determined **attempt.**

Success requires an intentional effort. She requires a completely new outlook, she requires a transformation, and in many cases a complete overhaul of what we have previously bought into.

This is a process by which we call 'The Untangling'.

Success says we are incompatible, hence why we never find her and even if we do, we cannot hold on to her.

Success says our basic design as human beings is fundamentally flawed if we desire to court her. Your biological make-up is set up for you to fail at tasks that would propel you to success or greatness.

You see, your brain's core responsibility outside of controlling your breathing, digesting your food and blood circulation, is simply designed to keep you alive. That's it.

The notion of keeping you alive, is contrary to the idea of success. Therefore you start to feel lethargic when a 'success' activity arises.

In order to keep you alive, your brain automatically rejects the 3 key words we mentioned above (achieve, process and effort).

Your brain by design, ejects 'action, exertion and attempt' from its workings. If your brain is anti-action, how the heck are you supposed to feel like pushing yourself outside of your comfort zone to capture success?

Your brain is like a dejected employee. It goes to work and does the bare minimum required in order to keep it's job, and if it is required to do more, it will require some form of motivation or compensation like an employee might.

Your brain is not designed to do overtime. It is simply designed to get on the train in the morning, work all day, get back on the train and sleep all night, rinse and repeat. Can you see any resemblances?

Your body, your mind is designed to protect you from pain. Effort, hard work, going beyond your comfort zone, is biological unhealthy for your body. Have you ever wondered why you never feel like working out, why you would rather watch YouTube than study, or why your mind automatically finds something much more interesting than working on your business?

Have you considered why we find chocolate more appealing than vegetable, or why we wince at criticism and find ourselves internally joyous at any tiny compliment?

Just like a computer game, you must discover or uncover the cheat codes that tricks your brain into going the extra mile.

Are you willing to start afresh? Are you ready to untangle?

Unfortunately, since your brain controls all functions, in order to achieve success or attain whatever goals you have set, you must learn to untangle your brain. Your brain will NEVER desire to work overtime, start a business, talk to the man or woman you have always found attractive.

Conversely, it will do one thing well and that is to ensure that you survive. However, survival is not good enough. Success is optimum. Success breeds socio and economic longevity, sustainability and legacy.

Failure to perform at an optimum level will result in eradication, devolution or and displacement in today's society thereby offering you as low hanging position on the economic and social ladder.

This book might be painful because we are going to navigate some sour home truths together. But trust me as your coach, by the time you finish reading this book, your perspective and mindset will have changed so dramatically that you will have all the truths, tools and wisdom to push you to your next level.

Are you ready for your 1st date with Success? She awaits

Can I be your mental gym instructor?

Do you give me permission to be brutally honest so we can sculpt the best version of you?

Will you allow me to seize your chocolate bar and sweets and every comfortable version of yourself that has been holding you back?

If you are truly ready to go on this journey with me. If you are willing to allow me to be brutal and push you to another level mentally and physically, beyond where you have ever been before, sign your name in Capital Letters below and date it.

Full Name

………………………………………………………………………………………..

Signature   **Date**

………………………………….   …………………………………....

"The road to success and the road to failure are almost exactly the same."

Colin R. Davis

Chapter II
Seeing is believing!

"Success loves a psychic. She says, if you can see the future, you will find me".

In my time as an entrepreneur, a mentor and a sales trainer, I have met, coached and talked with thousands of people, and anyone that manages to have a conversation with me, longer than 2 minutes would have been hit with a barrage of questions as part of my life long quest to discover the answer(s) to a very troubling question.

In a bid to uncover the 'secret' of success, a title often shrouded in mysticism or often only bestowed on the Mark Zuckerberg's, Richard Branson's or the Bill Gates' of the world, I have often wondered what the key ingredients were, that differentiated the high level achievers from the lower level achievers.

In my mind, successful people must operate, think, act and perform at a different level to most. They must do things a little different or perhaps see things through different lenses to most. What were the patterns or secrets?

To answer this burning question and in a bid to create a usable reference guide that anyone can follow, a toolbox of information that could turn anyone into a successful person if they followed the prescribed notions and findings, I needed to understand –

Why are some people successful and why are others not!

What really baffled me is that every single one of us desire success, yet not every single person attains it, therefore, it was not the desire to be successful that produced success.

Simply wanting something or wishing for something is evidently not the key to securing success.

Everyone assumes or are led to believe that hard work produced success, yet, real evidence proves against it. Builders, Cleaners, Nurses, are all some of the hardest working people in the world, yet we do not automatically ascribe success to them. So, there must be more to the tales of success.

In chapter one, *Success* introduced herself as havoc and in some cases, tumultuous but also as a thing that was willing to surrender to those who pursued her correctly or those knew how to handle her. No mention of the hardest worker.

To discover the truth of success. I found myself hanging out in club toilets in London, Mexico, New York, talking to the attendants, harassing tour guides in Columbia, nagging elephant sanctuary owners in Thailand, all the way to questioning CEOs of companies turning over anything from £10,000 to £30 million per annum. I found myself entrenched in debates, arguments and slanging matches, as this desire to understand why some people seem to win and why many seem to live a life of dissatisfaction.

In truth, this question mainly plagued me as an entrepreneur, who desired to find the best employees and partners for my businesses. I believed if someone understood what it required to be successful, if they knew the steps or strategies to tame success, then maybe they wouldn't need micro/macro management, they would be self-starters, no more pretending to pull a sickie after a night out, no more cajoling them to do their work, their standards would raise, their income would increase and therefore would improve their lives and businesses.

I spent countless hours trying to collate usable data that would exemplify why some people attain success and why some people settle at the lower tier. My first attempt at assimilating our findings failed because we asked a question that returned biases and therefore, we could not extrapolate any usable or objective data.

The two questions we asked are shown below -

1. Why is Bill Gates successful?
We received answers such as "because he is the wealthiest man on earth" or another prominent answer suggested he was successful because he did good for mankind. Both were equally correct. However, if we were to objectively determine how we could be successful, then we had to find another way of asking our questions.

2. What does success mean to you?
This led us nowhere. Most answers were vague and imprecise.

In order to understand what the differentiating factors between the successful and the unsuccessful, we collated further information from 967 people.

I chose to divide the data by asking two quantifiable questions

1. **On a scale of 1 to 10 - How successful would you say you are?**

I then placed anyone that ranked between 0-5 into group A and any persons that answered 6-10 into group B

We then asked - Group A (470 respondents) and Group B (497 respondents)- "Why are some people successful and why are some not?" **(Question 2)**

Group A	Group B
Given a leg up 27% Complacency 15% Nepotism 23% I don't know 26%	Work on yourself 17% **See the future before it happens 58%** They are selfish 19% Accept that no one is coming to rescue you 4%

We were happy with these questions. The answers were quantifiable and therefore we could gleam some useful data.

The results from Group A were really interesting. We discovered that those who ranked themselves lower than 5, saw things from a very different perspective to the respondents in Group B.

Group A's answers predicated that success was merely situational, nepotistic or lucky.

Furthermore 26% implied they did not know why some people were successful and why some were not.

The results from Group B really fascinated me. Their answers completely threw me off.

Work on yourself- 17%
See the future before it happens- 58%
They are selfish- 19%
Accept that no one is coming to rescue you- 4%

Throughout this book, I will be breaking down my research into these 4 super topics that play a part in pushing us to financial success. However, I am going to start with one that completely outranked the other answers.

See the future before it happens 58%

As an entrepreneur and business coach, I have always believed in the traditional keys to financial success such as hard work, smart investing, budgeting etc, however, I had never considered '*seeing the future before it happened*'.

In a bid to further understand what this really meant, I sent a follow up email to 497 Group B respondents and received 206 replies.

I asked, "In a short sentence, could you clarify what you mean by seeing the future before it happens?"

These were the responses

- Ability to see the goal in advance.
- Deep heart felt visualisation.
- Understanding what you desire to achieve before you have even started.
- Having a vision so you have a clear path to achieving it.

They all started with the end in mind. They knew what success looked like for them and then sought to achieve it.

Going back to chapter one. Remember your brain actively conspires against 'exertion, effort and action'. These successful people found a way to untangle their brain, by allowing it to see and believe that their goals were not contrary to the function of the brain. The process of seeing your goal, engaging your goal, breathing and smelling your goal, brings your brain closer to understanding it and therefore offers less resistance to achieving it.

They knew exactly what they wanted to the letter. This did not mean it happened how they envisaged it, but rather, they had something they could become obsessed over.

Life isn't wishy washy, or "let's see what happens tomorrow".

Life is real. Money is real. Dependants are real. The younger generation who are looking up to you are real as heck!

In a recent conversation with someone who scored 7 out of 10, he mentioned that most people do not even know what they are seeking and are just playing it by ear. He used the term 'winging it'. I had to ask what that meant, his reply stunned me. "Most people are throwing shit up against the wall and hoping it sticks" I got it straight away.

How do you expect to succeed if you don't know what success actually means to you?

I don't mean what success means, but what it means to **you** definitively and quantifiably.

Let me ask you right now- please prove me wrong!

What is **your** epitome of success?

Go.

List 5 of them

1.
2.
3.
4.
5.

If it took you more than 5 seconds to write them down, then the likely chance is that if you keep on this trajectory, that you will be a member of Group A.

I know it's the 1st chapter and maybe I should have eased you into my direct approach in a later chapter, but let us face it, indirectness has not worked so far, so let us try it my way. I am not here to sugar coat anything for you because something drastic needs to be done… TODAY!

If you want a cute, cuddly book to read, go pick up The Secret! and wish yourself into success. But I can promise you that if you stick with me till the end of this book, your life as you know it will change. You will become a beast; you will have power to achieve your goals; you will no longer play victim to your goals. I guarantee you will achieve 2x what you achieved in the last 12 months.

If my guarantee is not good enough for you… Burn the book!

58% see the future before it happens.
Before you can see the future and trick your brain into permitting it, you must understand what success really means to you first.

Success: the accomplishment of an aim or purpose.

So, before we can succeed, we must identify what aims and purposes are.

What do you want?
What does it look like?
How do I get there?

If you have no destination, how the heck are you going to get there? How the heck will you know when you get there? In fact, why the heck would you even get up from the lazy boy chair?

How often have you grabbed your car key, filled up the car to the brim with petrol, driven for 48 hours straight and then turned back home. NEVER right?! There is always an agenda. What is your life agenda?

Because in your normal life you set goals and benchmark the destination, but when it comes to the most important aspect of your life, you don't even buy petrol. You just drive aimlessly until the petrol (your energy) dies out, then we call the flipping RAC to come and rescue us.

Do you want to be successful YES or NO!

If you answered yes, let's talk for a moment. We need to create a plan for you so you can activate your brain to help you achieve it.

What is your life mission statement? A mission statement is simply a formal summary of the aims and values of a company or an individual. Mission statements are usually for stakeholders to understand where the company aims to go. We need to create a mission statement so that our greatest employee (our brain) can understand where you desire to go.

Every organisation or individual that desires to reach a destination must have a simple, succinct mission statement.

Have a browse below. I have noted four of the most successful businesses in the worlds' mission statement. These statements play testament to their success.

Facebook - "To give people the power to build community and bring the world closer together." (Turnover - $55 Billion Dollars, Impact – 2.2 Billion Active users (28.5% of the world's population)

BBC - To enrich people's lives with programmes and services that inform, educate and entertain." (Turnover – £4.9 Billion Pounds, Impact – 376 Million Weekly audience)

Uber - Uber's mission is to bring transportation — for everyone, everywhere (Turnover – £2.6 Billion Pounds, Impact – 15 Million Uber Trips daily)

Amazon – *"Our vision is to be earth's most customer-centric company; to build a place where people can come to find and discover anything they might want to buy online."* (Turnover – £232.88 billion dollars, Impact – 310 Million Customers)

Individuals

Steve Jobs - "To make a contribution to the world by making tools for the mind that advance humankind."

Oprah Winfrey - "To be a teacher. And to be known for inspiring my students to be more than they thought they could be."

What is your life mission statement/ What does success look like to you?

I have left some space below to write this……

Wealth

....
....
....
....
....

Health

....
....
....
....
....
....
....

Giving

....
....
....
....
....
....
....

Family

....
....
....
....
....

Business

....
....
....
....
....
....

If you want to be successful in something you must first have seen, smelt, heard, what that goal is. This is the fastest way to trick your brain to navigate toward it and give you an allowance to go and achieve it.

You must have all your faculties engaged in your material goals. If you desire a type of car then you must have written it down, test driven that car numerous times, listened to the engine roar, felt the comfort of the seat and have smelt the leather.

If you desire something specific, you MUST have seen, smelt, heard it and engaged all your senses and faculties before it can happen.

Your brain likes comfort. So, introduce your brain to your goals so it is familiar with it and not a stranger, so it can slowly start to allow you to work towards it.

Task to achieve:
Go to your life mission above
Go and engage all your 5 senses in that dream within the next week and develop a habit in doing it once or twice a month.

See
Taste
Feel
Smell
…your success before you can acquire it.

"Create a vision for the life you really want and then work relentlessly towards making it a reality."
Roy T. Bennett

Chapter III
The Disney Curse

Success love perseverance. She says, if you want to win, keep going!

The illustrious story by The Brothers Grimm, Rapunzel, tricked us into believing a world where a prince, a rescuer, a saviour of some sort would magically hear of our woes and come to our rescue. Call me the grinch, a grouch, a party pooper, in fact, call me whatever you want, but these fancy narratives have played a dangerous role in why we are where we are right now!

Let's look back at a snippet of the famous story that each and every single child is taught during our impressionable years.

'it came to pass that <u>the Prince rode through the forest</u> and went by the tower. <u>He happened to hear a song which was so lovely that he stood still and listened</u>. This was Rapunzel who in her loneliness passed her time singing. The Prince wanted to climb up to her, and looked for the door of the tower, but none was to be found. He rode home, <u>but the singing had so deeply touched his heart, that every day he went out into the forest and listened to it</u>'

We have become conditioned to believing that if we are good people, if we are honest and abide by the law, do nice things, then by some sort of virtue, someone or something, will be our saving grace. We have unconsciously become accustomed to the notion that someone will be available to help in our uttermost time of need.

I researched deeper into the ideas and psychology that held people back from producing results at the higher echelon or achieving success at higher levels.

The results scared me so much that I did a double take at my research.

I laughed at myself and had to run my ideas past my team. What I discovered would see me laughed out of schools, homes and presentations in front of my high esteemed peers. Either way, I'm going to tell you.

I am going to tell you why you are not at the level that you desire to be. Why you have not achieved the goals you wanted to achieve.

There were several reasons, but one really struck a chord with me.

It's because of Rapunzel, Cinderella and Snow White. Now, I know I might sound like a scrooge, but understand that we are products of our childhoods, we are products of our past hood; we *are* the information we have believed.

The information we garnered as children, play a significant role in our behaviours, attitude, mindset and aspirations, even today.

What we are 'fed' as kids, nearly always manifests itself in some form during later aspects of our adult lives. If you are led to believe that you are useless as a child, psychologist have proven that this will manifest in some form in your adult life.

If we are fed [led] to believe that someone, will come to rescue us due to no effort on our part or a saviour will save us with no external effort from us, then it is a recipe for disaster. Many of us have never pushed ourselves outside of our comfort zones because unconsciously we 'think' we will be ok. That just maybe, if we fall then someone or a system will prop us back up.

II

Can I be brutally honest? Because, this might just change your life!

I spend my down time watching a lot of murder cases and hostage negotiations programs on Netflix. Don't judge me. I guess we all have our vices. Mine happens to be kidnap, murder, hostages, and lots of blood and brain matter splattered all over the floor. The hostage series always makes me giggle, not because some poor soul has been held captive against their wishes, but more because it's a reminder that life is a big bag of dog excrement. In almost all hostage situations on television, especially in the rise of Netflix, hostages are always rescued, ransoms are paid, demands negotiated, big bad scary terrorists are killed to rescue little old you. These hostage television shows are a 100% attributed to why you are where you are today.

We are taught, fed, led to believe that someone is coming to free and rescue you. That in your time of need or distress, a superman, a batman, a tactical hostage negotiator is risking everything to free you. Does this remind you of a certain Rapunzel or Snow White?

There is always a scene where an officer or investigator, draws out a diagram depicting how they intend to extract the hostage from a hostage situation. They plan to drop rope through a 15-storey building window, throw in a stun grenade, temporarily incapacitate the terrorist(s) and shoot them dead.

In some cases, they gallantly plan, strategise, negotiate, consider ransom demands and occasionally, hand over large cases of money to the kidnappers, in order to rescue a hostage.

We have built up this narrative, this unspoken belief, that we are somewhat worthy of saving. That one brave person will take up the mantle, don their shiny knight amour and come to our rescue.

Look, nobody is coming to rescue you. You are in this race and journey by yourself and every opportunity you take is created by you. When was the last time someone came and handed you a suitcase full of cash? When was the last time someone heard of your woes and came and sorted it for you? Every opportunity you don't take is a detriment to you. When you start to accept that everything and anything you need in this life is derived from the works of your hands then you have passed level 1.

We are too fluffy.

Nobody wants to accept that our flaws, our sentiments, our insecurities are holding us back from attain our goals. We hide behind our irresponsible friend who cheers us on from our bad, destructive habits. We shy away and get offended by those who dare to be real about some of your hindering character traits. In fact, we title them haters. What if they are right? What if they are correct? What if they can see a clearer and more accurate image of us?

Nobody is sitting in their garage plotting a tactical offense on how they will rescue you. Only you can do it.

ACTION:

Go into your quiet space. Pull out a piece of paper and write down how you intend to escape this self-imposed hostage situation you have found yourself in.

You walked into a bank.
You saw masked gun men
You stood still when everyone ran
What are you going to do to escape because right now you are stuck!

It starts with having a candid and honest conversation with yourself. It starts with accepting that you are solely responsible for where you are today.

It starts with you. You are responsible for the amount of money you have in your pocket right now.

It starts with, you are responsible for your current state of happiness.

You hold the keys to the door of your liberation.

Pull out another piece of paper – title it 'I am' and note down all your negative attributes. Don't stop until you hit at least 10 things.

This will be hard. When was the last time you had to face self-criticism? We all prefer to hear the cute, little nice things about ourselves. When was the last time someone told you, you had a great smile and you stopped smiling? We accentuate and push forward our positive attributes. Yet, we can only start to change for the better when we hear the truth about our character flaws. Since your friends and family haven't got the guts to tell you truths about yourself. You are going to have to do this yourself.

Do not move on to the next page until we fight these demons. Today is the day we discover who we really are and what has been holding us back from our successes.

FACE IT HEAD ON! Pretending there is no problem will not make the problem go away.

Let me show you mine first

I am……….
Lazy
Unable to take criticism
A serial procrastinator
Bad with money
I am extremely defensive
I feel like I am better than others
I am scared about my future
I am impatient
I jump from idea to idea
Complacent

What are yours….

I am
1.
2.
3.
4.
5.
6.
7.
8.
9.
10.

I had to have a real conversation with myself.
1. I am lazy and therefore I do not achieve my full potential
2. I am unable to take criticism and therefore I am unable to grow

What are the consequences of these flaws you have put down?
1.
2.
3.
4.
5.
6.
7.
8.
9.
10.

Once you understand the impact of these flaws and how they are holding you back from achieving your goals, then actively tackle them and move one step closer to living a more fulfilled life.

You see, it is not our parents' fault. They did an incredible job by introducing us to the magical world of story, creativity, dreams and free thinking. However, once you start to understand how our current decisions, our perspectives, our mindset, our current circumstances are based on an amalgamation of information we were force fed or narrative we chose to buy into, then we realise that until we face them head on we will continue to have the same results we have been having.

"Don't be afraid to give up the good to go for the great."

John D. Rockefeller

Chapter IV
Punish Your non-commitments

Success loves integrity. She says, if you say you are going to do something, then bloody do it. She accepts no excuses.

Do you remember the last promise you broke? Can you still remember how the person you promised felt? Can you remember the look in their eyes, the look of disdain, mistrust, and utter disappointment?

The psychology of a promise is greater than just the uttered words, but more about the trust of character, the heightened integrity, the willingness to be vulnerable and the embracement of hope when someone offers us a promise, a vow or simply their word. Hence why the feeling of disappointment is so poignant when someone breaks a promise to us.

A broken promise, regardless of how small it's perceived, has enough power to destroy nations through wars, dissolve marriages through unfaithfulness, demolish friendships through a lack of integrity.

When a promise is made, psychologists suggests, we tend to lower our nature created self-protective guard, because a promise acts as a form of surety, it acts as a guarantee and therefore encourages us to bypass our critical factors, lower our intense need to stay on guard and therefore we trust more, we love more, we allow ourselves to be more vulnerable. However, if that promise if broken, Carthen and Woode's research on social attachment showed, that humans feel abused or victimised as we feel our trust has therefore been stolen from us.

Our premise as mere humans, survives on upheld promises, vow, oaths and guarantees. If our promises were never upheld, we would suffer civil crisis, wars, riots and such, as there would be no accountability for any unspent promises.

In our society, a broken promise often leads to distrust, lack or loss of credibility, causes upset and most importantly destroys kinship towards us, simply because society suggests that our strongest bond is our words and our promises.

Imagine a world where no one was held accountable for the promises or commitments they make. In fact, imagine a society, where we could say whatever we desire, yet not be held accountable if we failed to keep our words.

The notion of a promise is what our society is built on. The promise to protect our family, the promise to keep our vows in marriage, our promises not to neglect our children just because they constantly annoy us. Promises are what sociologist call 'social glues.' It's the bond that holds everything together, hence, the consequences associated with breaking them is great.

We put in so much effort to ensure our integrity is intact because we never want to be perceived as a promise breaker.

We surveyed 94 married men and women and asked them two questions

1. Would you consider yourself to be an honest person?
2. How often would you say you kept a promise to your spouse?

Men	Women

Would you consider yourself to be an honest person? (89% YES)	Would you consider yourself to be an honest person? (92% YES)
How often would you say you kept a promise to your spouse? (94%)	How often would you say you kept a promise to a spouse? (97%)

Look at the figures, people will do anything to be perceived as an honest, promise keeping person, especially to someone they care about.

Let me ask you a question
Do you keep most of your promises?
What percentage of your promises do you keep?

My question to you is that why do we put so much effort into ensuring we keep our promises to each other, yet we routinely break our promises and commitments to ourselves?

If you want to be successful. Then you have to learn how to keep a promise to yourself.

We disrespect ourselves so often and often overlook our behaviours. If we were another person, would we tolerate the untold promises, lies, commitments we have broken? Of course, we wouldn't. So why should we accept it from ourselves?

You made internal vows to yourself to read and complete a book, yet you did not do it!

You made a promise to yourself to start a business, yet you find yourself making excuses!

You vowed to change your life, but you are still in the same place as you were 5 years ago!

Let me ask you a question. If these promises were promises you made to others, would you have had more impetus to fulfil them? Of course, you would.

The fundamental issue is that there are no immediate consequences to our inactions, which is why we put off our goals and we therefore do not achieve success. We constantly break the vows and promises we've made to ourselves.

So, let us stop pretending to the world that we are creatures of integrity when we don't fulfil our duties to ourselves.

From today we will start by punishing our broken promises to ourselves. Such as there are consequences for breaking promises to our friends, family and society. There must be consequences for inaction or broken promises to ourselves.

Why should we reward our success, yet we fail to punish failure? This again is evidence of our desire to run away from the realities of life. You want a pat on the back from doing something that will enhance your life, yet you don't want the punch in the face for not doing something that you made a commitment to do, that would have also enhanced your life.

You see, why I'm harsh. How does that even make sense?! You want the reward but don't want the punishment.

If you really desire to succeed. Start punishing the commitments you do not keep. There must be consequences!

Let's start immediately. Remember you signed that form in Chapter 1 to allow me to push you to the next level.

No more games…

When I was writing my book '6 zeros before 30', I put up £3000 pounds to a community of 5000 people. I asked anyone who has always disliked me or wanted my money to tag themselves in the post. If I failed to complete and publish the book by 26th July. I would pick a random person and give them the £3000. Guess what happened! After months of procrastination and laziness, I finished the book in 2 months. The fear of losing my hard-earned money due to laziness, pushed me far beyond what I would have accomplished if there was no consequence.

Over the next 24 hours, write down the goals you want to achieve in the next 12 months, using this format.

Goals

1.
2.
3.
4.
5.

What are the direct consequences for not pushing yourself or achieving the goal you set out?

Goals	Punishment

Then send an email to an honest friend or post the above box on social media

There must be consequences.

In the workplace there are consequences for not doing what we are supposed to do.
In the household there are consequences for not bringing home the bacon.

We never consider the consequence for our inactions simply because they are usually future consequences, therefore it is not an immediate impact, so you can keep **forgoing** it. But it changes today.

Today will be the last day you fail to punish yourself for not doing what you set out to do.

When we punish ourselves it forces us to…

1. Reassess

2. Strategize

3. Learn

When was the last time you reassessed things after a win? Failure is the biggest teacher in life. Every successful person will tell you that failing in something completely changed their life or perspective.

"If you are not willing to risk the usual, you will have to settle for the ordinary."

Jim Rohn

Chapter V
Become selfish

Success loves attention. She says, if you say you are going to pursue me, then make sure I am the only one. I am a jealous lover.

Every child around the age of 2 goes through the 'my', 'mine' or 'me' phase, where everything they touch seemingly belongs to them. A toy, your pen, someone else's food or item, seems to automatically become theirs.

And guess what, every single parent, grandparent or pre-school teacher does?

We use that opportunity to teach that child that 'selfishness' is a bad trait, we encourage them to share with others people, in fact, we go one step further, we encourage the child, not only to share, but give the toy to the other child, because good children put others before themselves. And I agree. Children should learn the importance of selflessness, so they do not because annoying little brats as they grow up.

As a parent or guardian, I want to commend you on instilling such important traits in us. Well done, for teaching us the right way and I am sure, that one day when I become a parent, I will also teach my children the value of kindness and sharing.

However, on this quest to success, we must reshuffle some ideas, we must reassess some teachings and rejig some prior understandings. As of right now, as an adult, we need to scrap this seemingly great habit of selflessness that we have adopted and do the complete opposite.

Yes, I am vying for the abandonment of selflessness and the adoption of selfishness.

This might sound a little troubling especially in a 'self-development' book, but trust me, it's just a much-needed temporary measure.

We are products of our education and upbringing. Second place has seeped into your bloodstream and killed your competitive nature. To achieve success, you need to develop a one-track mind instead of trying to carry the entire world on your back. It is so dangerous. We carry everyone, we put every person's goals, feelings, desires first and end up spreading ourselves too thin to even pursue our goals.

Listen! We are not kids anymore, yet we still play by the same rules. We have big goals, we have responsibilities, we have targets that need to be achieved and it requires you to drop this 'I am the saviour complex', 'I am going to rescue the world' or even 'I must put everyone before me' nonsense and become selfish.

Your plane is about to crash. Please brace for impact! What do you do? Do you follow the instruction you were given at the beginning of the flight or do you ignore it?

"Please place your oxygen mask over your face first before you assist anyone". What use are you to others if you are incapable of helping because you have passed out.

Let's try that analogy again. Life is shitty right? Things are not going as well as they should. Do you dedicate your entire being and resources to putting others first or empowering yourself so you can serve others better?

In fact, its' selfish to not have enough resources so you can eventually bless others.

SUCCESS requires all your attention

How much of yourself can you give when you only have a small % left for yourself.

In some families, your family breakthrough is depending on you going out there, breaking the mould, shattering the status quo and leading the pack.

If you are broken, if you are helpless, how helpful will you or can you be to others.

We make the mistake of spreading ourselves too thin as we try to help everyone. If your pockets are empty, how do you feed others.

Many of you will struggle with this selfishness theory but once you try it out for a month. Put yourself first for 30 days and see the results you will yield.

Stop trying to carry a village, when you are the only hunter. The hunter needs space, time to hunt, gather his/her thought, strategize, to provide and protect the village.

Putting yourself first is intended to open the gates for others. It might come across as a 'selfish' act but in fact, it's the opposite. It is your way of opening the eyes of the people that rely on you to wake up, watch you set an example and make them realise that they can also be self-sufficient. Let's look back to Roger Bannister, the first man to break a seemingly impossible task. Roger ran a 4 minute mile in 3:58.8 minutes.

Many had attempted this and failed, but once Roger did it, 6 weeks later John Landy did it. After Landy, just a year later, three runners broke the four-minute barrier *in a single race*. Over the last half century, more than a thousand runners have conquered a barrier that had once been considered hopelessly out of reach.

Sir Roger Bannister should serve as an example to everyone. Bannister is recognised as an innovator, a change agent. Your selfishness could be what liberates your staff, your family, your generation. Your version of a 4-minute mile run might be just what the world needs to see.

In 1968 Jim Hines was the first to break the 10 second 100m sprint, after him 136 others have achieved this including Usain Bolt, who ran it at 9.76 seconds.

Many of the people you are carrying don't even need your help, they just need to see someone get out of the gates and win.

Ps: Only become selfish, if you can make a solemn promise or dedication that you will come back and rescue everyone.

"Your beliefs become your thoughts,
Your thoughts become your words,
Your words become your actions,
Your actions become your habits,
Your habits become your values,
Your values become your destiny."
Gandhi

Chapter VI
The Power of Right Now

Success requires belief. She says, if you want me, then you have to make sure I am the only thing on your mind. Clear your mind

We have some things to deal with if we want to catch success. She can only date someone who has space for her. She is unwilling to share your mind with others. Success is a jealous lover. She says, "I will not allow someone else to share your brain space".

She says we need to delete all the other girls' numbers from your mind's phone. You must delete the files of your exes from your computer. I do not share. I either dominate or I leave it to someone else. You choose. I do not compete.

You have get rid of the shit in your head.

If you truly desire to achieve those things you noted in chapter 1, then we need to start by brainwashing ourselves. Yes, we need to change the way we think about success, but more importantly we must change the way we think about ourselves. This is what I called THE UNTANGLING.

There are stories, ideas, images about ourselves that we have built up. We have bought into ideas about who we are, what we are and what we are capable of doing.

These thoughts are so dangerous and from speaking to 100+ high level achievers, we gathered that you can desire to be successful, you can want to be a millionaire, you can have all sort of crazy goals, but until The Untangling occurs, you will never fulfil your goals.

We are sponges and soak in everything we are told about ourselves and this started since we were kids. Some were led to believe they were terrible at physical sports. Some of us were told (made to believe) as kids that we are terrible at maths so guess what happened? We steered clear of maths and shied away from numbers. Do you think we would opt to do a degree in mathematics? And as we grow up our decisions are based on the ideas and notions we have believed. Our beliefs systems are created from when we are young and often created by those people who could not achieve, and in the spirit of protecting us from failures, they imposed their fears on us.

I want you to start thinking back right now.

What were you told about:
Money
Love
Wealth
Your looks
Your size

Before we can even start to talk about success, we have to talk about something first. Do you even believe you can be successful? It might sound like a really simple question, but you have to pull yourself aside and ask yourself this question. Do you really believe you are even allowed to be successful?

I feel it is important to use this section wisely because you will NEVER outperform what you believe about yourself.

Let us start The Untangling by adopting affirmations, conversations, public declarations, repetitions.

Take a few moments out to ask yourself, what are some of things you believe about yourself that are not positive and let's address them together.

You will never succeed in business unless we deal with these things right here and right now.

We have to untangle some spoken and unspoken narratives. These are often referred to as Limiting Beliefs. Self-limiting beliefs are assumptions or perceptions that have about yourself and about the way the world works.

Many limiting beliefs are not your fault. What is your fault is if you carry on the narrative and pass them down to children and others.

We develop beliefs that become our guiding systems and principles. For example, if you were told you were not great at football over and over, your brain may start to collate this information as your truth. Let me guarantee you that today you would not be playing football.

We have to identify your internal conversations and untangle them.

What are some of the negative self-beliefs?

These usually start with 'I' or 'I am'. Sometimes they are spoken aloud, but many a times they are silent, tiny voices in your mind, which make up how you believe and eventually behave.

Do these thoughts or words resonate with you?

I am not worth anything

I am boring

Nobody cares about me

I am not good enough

I am no good

I never come first

I always fail

I always come second

I'm not valuable

I am unimportant

I'm not anybody

I am incompetent

I am disposable

I can't achieve

I can't change

How do you break away from these thoughts and words?

1. Identify one belief at a time – Catch the thought and quickly write it down.

2. Understand how it impacts your life.

TIP – Discover several ways to disprove these core belief. You must replace the idea with another idea.

For example - I am always making mistakes. Pull out your book and note down every time you have not made a mistake for the next week.

Nobody likes me. Pull out the book and write down every time someone actually liked you.

Good Luck

Author's Note

Success loves Strategy! Be strategic.

Anyone can be successful. It just requires a strategy.

Good Luck

Your mentor,
TJ Atkinson

Printed in Great Britain
by Amazon